# EARLY UTAH FURNITURE

## BY CONNIE MORNINGSTAR

Utah State University Press, Logan, Utah

Copyright © 1976, Utah State University Press

**Library of Congress Cataloging in Publication Data**

Morningstar, Connie, 1927-
Early Utah Furniture.

Includes index.
1. Furniture, Mormon—Utah. 2. Furniture—Utah.
3. Cabinet-workers—Utah—Directories.  I. Title.
NK2435.U8M67     749.2'192     76-29637
ISBN 0-87421-088-7

Anyone ought to be able to describe a chair. But given the peculiarities of frontier furniture making, one picture is indeed worth a thousand words. This work would have been many thousands of words longer but for the photographs provided by my husband, Gale Morningstar. Although he would much rather take pictures of mountains and sunsets, all photos not otherwise credited are his.

For both of us, this project provided a fascinating study of a heretofore neglected subject. It was over a year in the works and covered an area from Logan to the Arizona Strip. Much time was spent at the Historical Society library in Salt Lake and much appreciation is due the helpful and patient librarian, Martha Stewart. For permitting us to photograph furniture items in their homes, we're indebted to John Edwards, Willard; Mr. and Mrs. George Wilcox, Layton; Ralph Ramsay's two charming granddaughters in Richfield, Melissa Cluff and Ettene Ramsay; and the Kenneth J. Capelles of Brigham City, the latter collectors and restorers of early Utah pine furniture and, like ourselves, relative newcomers to the state.

Jon Sweet wrestled heavy furniture and seemed unperturbed when we re-arranged his Salt Lake shop, Honest Jon's, for just the right photo of a particularly interesting old piece.

Lois Lang, at the time curator of the Brigham Young and Jacob Hamblin homes in St. George and Santa Clara, respectively, was most helpful in permitting us to photograph furnishings therein. Jim Guilliam was a well-informed guide to these homes which were then owned by the Utah State Parks and Recreation Department. Our appreciation also to the National Parks Service for information and freedom to photograph Utah-made furniture at Pipe Spring National Monument in Arizona.

Finally, our thanks to Donald T. Schmidt, Church Librarian-Archivist, for supplying very pertinent information about elusive cabinetmakers and to Florence S. Jacobsen, Church Curator, for providing photographs of furniture items owned by the LDS Church.

Connie VanOrden Morningstar
Murray, Utah
September 1976

It was make-do-with-what-you-have necessity that dictated furniture production in early Utah settlements. Pieces were functional, unadorned, and stylistically indistinguishable from the "country" furniture of New England and the north-central states in that first half of the 19th century.

Styles lingered longer in the Mountain West because of the area's isolation, perhaps, and furniture with a decided Empire or Sheraton Fancy flavor was produced there long after Victorian styles had taken hold elsewhere. With the possible exception of the Mormon couch, no uniquely regional pieces or designs developed. Yet good construction and ingenuity overcame poor raw materials, and realistic graining and marbleizing became a honed art endowing with a particular character those pieces produced in the relatively short time between the coming of the Mormons in 1847 and the coming of the railroad in 1869.

The average Mormon pioneer was a bit different from the stereotyped western frontiersman in aspects other than religious. He was an Anglo by way of New England, for the most part, although this generalization is quickly tempered by the fact that a hundred Mississippians met the original company and entered the Salt Lake valley with them on July 24, 1847. He was a tradesman or craftsman — a town-dweller rather than a homesteader. If he happened to be a farmer (and many became so of necessity), he lived in town and went out to his fields daily. Many had gained experience with theocracy from living in the Mormon settlement of Nauvoo, Illinois. And most soon became furniture makers of sorts.

On August 3, 1847, ten days after the first company entered the valley, Howard Egan wrote in his journal, "J. Redding and myself went this morning with a team 8 miles up the pass within a mile of the last camping site where we cut down and brought to camp two cedars for purposes of making bedsteads, pails, etc."

A few treasured pieces of furniture might have been brought across the plains, but for the most part seed, foodstuffs, and tools were more important and any furniture would be makeshift. Families slept in the wagons that brought them at first. Then with the log cabin erected or the dug-out entrenched, a bedstead was built into a corner — sprung with ropes or rawhide strips and mattressed with a straw tick. Chest tops doubled as tables, if one was lucky enough to own a chest. Otherwise, planks laid across sections of logs served as well.

The earliest known Utah-made chair extant is a four-slat ladderback rocker of juniper taken from Little Cottonwood Canyon, about fifteen miles southeast of Salt Lake City, during the winter of 1847-1848. It was made by Charles Sperry for Mrs. Mary Pitchforth. It has a woven rawhide thong seat and is stained dark red. One of the amateurs perhaps, Charles Sperry doesn't surface again in news of the trade.

The bane of Utah furniture manufacturing, then as now, was the dearth of fine hardwoods. The mountains and canyons to the east and west of the valley abounded in timber — juniper (often called cedar), white pine, quaking aspen (asp), red pine, and cottonwood. But roads and bridges being what they were, lumbering was somewhat difficult. Howard Egan concludes his account of that August 3rd foray: "We arrived at home about 9 in the evening. We had quite a hard time of it, the roads being almost impassable on account of the bridge having floated off."

Even so, before the end of 1847, a sawmill was set up in Bingham Canyon in the Oquirrh range on the west of the valley. Two more were established on Mill Creek southeast of Salt Lake City the following year. And by 1853, there were over a hundred sawmills in operation throughout the Territory. While shingles and siding were the principal products, many of these mills were soon also producing furniture or the turned members for furniture construction.

Cabinetmakers and furniture dealers trailed their advertisements with lists of woods wanted in exchange. H. W. Naisbett advised in 1857 that he would accept "scrip, wood, lumber, produce &c." in exchange for furniture. The following year, he wrote, "I am prepared to supply Flour Boxes made of good seasoned lumber at reasonable prices. For those who supply their own material, I will make up Boxes at a low figure."

About the same time, J. C. Little wanted "10 cords Quaking-asp Timber & 10,000 feet of lumber of various kinds" for which he would pay in "Furniture, Chairs, and City Scrip." As late as 1865, Henry Dinwoodey requested 100,000 feet of lumber "one-inch white pine, 4x4 inch white pine scantling (for turned members), 3x4 inch white and red pine scantling, and two-inch Cottonwood plank (for seats)."

Upholstery materials were in short supply during the pioneer period, so chair bottoms customarily were plank — sometimes rolled in the Boston rocker manner; sometimes with a shallow depression scooped out of the flat seat. Rush seats were common. So were those made of rawhide — either single pieces stretched across seat and back or thin strips or thongs woven in an open pattern.

Early ladderback chairs were indeed primitive at best. But as soon as the immediate need had been satisfied, Utah pieces were the equal of simple furniture in the Country Empire, Sheraton Fancy, or Windsor styles produced elsewhere at the time. Professional cabinetmakers, most of whom had served apprenticeships in England, appeared on the scene and furniture manufacture moved from the province of the householder to the province of the cabinetshop.

The usual progression of furniture styles in America was from England to the eastern urban areas to the midwest, hence westward. Exceptions were the Anglo settlements in California which received shipments of furniture almost as soon as such pieces were available on the Atlantic coast. But in any case, the intermountain region was the last to get creations in the latest fashion. This ordinarily orderly progression was leap-frogged by the Mormon Church's proclivity for gathering its new converts to Zion in the Salt Lake valley.

In the spring of 1854, William Bell came directly to Utah (via the port of New Orleans) from his native England where he had been, for twenty years, an expert cabinetmaker in London. The result was that his furniture pieces showed influence of early Victorian designs. These included secretaries and wardrobes bearing distinct Victorian Gothic motifs, a style that was then beginning to catch on in the eastern states but was years away from the western frontier. The inlaid octagon-top pedestal table for example, similar to one Bell created for the 1858 Territorial fair, was known in England about 1840; and his Morris-type chair made for Heber C. Kimball probably in the 1860s predates the general acceptance of this design in America by some twenty years.

The double or single lounge, a sofa-bed which has since become known as the Mormon couch, was a characteristic piece and was produced by most early Utah cabinetshops. The lounges usually were about six feet long with a seat too deep for comfortable sitting. Arms and back were of equal height and usually were composed of turned vertical spindles, often with a scrolled crest and arms in the Empire manner. The platform consisted of wooden slats parallel to the arms over which was placed a cushion or folded comforter.

Double lounges had an extra pair of front legs and slats which alternated with those in the platform. This section could be pulled forward to make a double bed. In some areas, these were called Bishop's couches—ready on short notice to accommodate an extra guest or two overnight.

Information at this writing seems to indicate this piece is a Mormon design. Similar couches have been found in Missouri and Illinois, but the Saints were in both places before the exodus to Utah. However, a backless day bed known to have been made in Texas in the 1860s employs the same extension principle as the double lounge.

The Dixie rocker, an interpretation of the familiar Boston rocker, apparently was turned out by cabinetshops throughout the Territory, but most of them have been found in the St. George area of Utah's Dixie. These are generally attributed to the Builders' Union, a group of craftsmen who gained experience building the St. George Temple and Tabernacle and afterward applied this expertise to the construction of homes and fine furniture. The rockers were made of local Ponderosa pine and are characterized by three to six contoured back bannisters, each about one inch square, and heavy, turned, splayed legs which grip thin rockers in clothespin style. Seats are plank, often shaped. Dark red stain or paint was the usual finish.

Flour boxes were a standard kitchen item produced everywhere. They were large utilitarian pieces, capable of holding 1,000 pounds of flour (or wood, if one preferred) and were undecorated except for an occasional scrolled skirt. As was the case for most pieces, an earthy red stain was the common finish.

Rush-bottomed chairs with decorative ball-shaped spacers between the back slats, variations of Sheraton Fancies, appeared frequently and many have been attributed to Brigham Young, his cabinetshop or drawing board. Brigham Young was, by trade, a glazier (paint-finisher, in this case) and chairmaker. As a young man in 1829, he built a two-story workshop-home on a stream in Mendon, New York. Living quarters were on the second floor and the main level contained his shop where chairs and spinning wheels were made. The lathe was powered by a water wheel. It is interesting to note that Sheraton Fancies, many with this particular decorative detail, were extremely popular in rural America at that time and many were known to have been made in west-central New York. Brigham Young's cabinetshop in Nauvoo, Illinois, also produced items in the style of the period, the sale of which supported his family while Young served a church mission to England.

It seems logical to assume (and church historians insist) that Brigham Young as president of the Church and governor of the Territory was much too busy to design, let alone construct, furniture after arriving in Utah. Nevertheless, the legends die hard and one of them claims that he would occasionally spend an evening in his shop "just to keep his hand in." After 1854, the shop was operated by William Bell who for some years made furniture exclusively for the Young families.

The Public Works project on Temple Block was begun in January 1850 under the direction of the LDS Church First Presidency with Daniel H. Wells as superintendent. Here nearly all immigrant craftsmen worked until they found private employment. A carpenter shop, blacksmith shop, machine shop (where mill and other equipment was manufactured), and a paint shop were among the first units established. Carpenters and builders were under the foremanship of Miles Romney.

Few items of Utah-made furniture were labeled, but at least some chairs produced in the Public Works cabinetshop bear a brand reading, "Public Works/G.S.L.C." and the date of manufacture. The initials, incidentally, stand for Great Salt Lake City, the official name of the settlement.

Wages at the Public Works were paid in scrip which could be redeemed at the Tithing Office for most of the necessities of life. And in a community where barter was the usual and accepted medium of exchange, Public Works scrip was generally accepted as legal tender in private commercial establishments as well.

While Public Works provided initial or emergency employment, private endeavor was always encouraged and stimulated by such means as the awards granted at the annual fair of the Deseret Agricultural and Manufacturing Society (D.A.&M.). In the furniture category of the October 1860 fair, Jesse C. Little walked off with first-place honors and $3 each for the best sofa and best bureau. Best six-chairs award ($3) went to John Cottam who also won $2 for the best rocking chair. Ralph Ramsay received $2 for the best specimen of wood carving, a mantlepiece.

Categories the following year included best bureau, sofa, bedstead, six chairs, center table, dining table, ladies' work stand, office desk, rocking chair, writing desk; and the best specimen of wood carving, wood turning, and French polishing. Following the exhibit, Edward Hunter, president, announced that "the display of furniture was highly creditable to the several manufacturers. In this as in every other department, we could discern the manifestations of increased wealth in the community, demanding the expenditure of extra labor and ingenuity, on the several appliances for domestic comfort and convenience, while the gradual development of beauty in countless channels marks the drawing of an era far in advance of strict necessity and comparative poverty."

Things were indeed looking up. The September 7, 1864, **Deseret News** carried a cabinetmaker's revised list of prices for furniture. These "moderate" prices in gold or its equivalent were established by mutual approval of local cabinetmakers:

Common bedstead, $14
Right square bedstead, $16; screws
    and slats added. $3
Crib, $10
Windsor chair, $3
Rush bottom chair, $2
Child's highchair, $3
French chair, $5
Sewing chair, $5

Congress (captain's) chair, $5
Large rocking chair, $9
Lounge, turned post, $11
Lounge, scrolled, $14
Lounge, double, scrolled, $16
Center table, 3½ feet in diameter, $26
Round stand, medium, $6
Wash stand with drawer, $10

Whether or not Brigham Young personally made furniture in Utah, his influence on its decoration is unquestioned. His technique for simulating wood graining was so characteristic that the result was often referred to as "Brigham Oak." The effect was achieved by the use of metal combs, feathers, brushes, or simply bare knuckles.

This use of paint and talent to give native pine the appearance of oak, mahogany, birdseye maple, burled walnut, or marble was applied to wall panels, mantles, all kinds of furniture — even pillars such as the massive ones inside the Salt Lake Tabernacle. In the early days, however, good paint was hard to come by and, as a consequence, many pieces were simply seasoned in the smokehouse then rubbed with oil. Often a milk or buttermilk base paint was used which was colored dark red with blood — a readily available ingredient at slaughtering time. Or Utah's colorful red earth would be mixed with lard to the desired shade, then rubbed into the wood for an interesting (and enduring) stain.

By 1854 when some commercial paint was available, a meeting was called for "considering the propriety of establishing uniform charges for all kinds of painting, glazing, &c. throughout the Territory." A proposed price list was submitted to Brigham Young for his approval, which was granted. The rate for graining oak, mahogany, rosewood, etc., was set at $2 per yard. For marbling mantlepieces, $4 to $6. Blue paint was $1.25 a pound; greens and yellows, $1.50. Vermillion, red, "lake," etc. were extra.

Valley citizens were regularly admonished to grow flax so the seeds might be used for paint manufacture. Brigham Young's sermons often extolled the virtues of the flaxseed paint produced at the Public Works plant noting that the local product was as good, if not better, than any that could be bought in the States.

Still, proper ingredients posed a problem. In a spring swing through the southern counties early in 1861, George A. Smith and Joseph A. Young observed that the prosperous citizens of Minersville had erected a new smelting furnace, but it seemed that they were having difficulty getting lead out "either because they lacked the means to carry on the business successfully or from some other cause not reported. The lead is said to be very easy of access, and the ore exceedingly rich; and if those now engaged in the business do not or cannot make it profitable, others should take hold and smelt out a sufficiency of lead to supply the market at prices that will exclude importation, and so low that some enterprising person or company may be induced to commence the manufacture of paints, for which there is and will be a great and increasing demand."

It was the same with nails. Early in 1857, the **Deseret News** had advised that "D. Sabin has machinery in operation for making all kinds of nails to order." In 1860, the **News** reported that the nail factory of the Messrs. Sabin, Beebe & Co., Payson, was doing good work and that the Messrs. Adams, Grace & Co. at Nephi were also engaged in the manufacture of nails. The Iron Mission in the Cedar City area of central Utah was established primarily for the production of nails, but it met with a series of failures.

Machinery for the manufacture of nails and screws became available in Salt Lake City in 1859 and was used to process surplus iron brought in by the federal troops who occupied Utah from 1858-1861.* Some excellent cut nails in assorted sizes, presumed to be from President Wells' factory (Public Works?) and several trays of assorted wrought nails were exhibited at the D.A.&M. fair in October 1861. The supply of scrap ran out by 1865, however, and a nail shortage existed until the coming of the railroad four years later.

---

* President James Buchanan sent an army detachment of some 3,000 men under the command of Colonel (later General) Albert Sidney Johnston to Utah Territory in 1857 to put down a supposed Mormon uprising. The army wintered in Emigration Canyon, then passed peacefully through the shuttered city the following spring and established Camp Floyd about 35 miles to the southwest where it remained until 1861.

So any substitute for nails was welcome in the early days. Rawhide seats and backs helped. Rawhide — a single piece, strips, or thongs — was first soaked then attached to the side rails and stretched or woven to form the seat. As the rawhide dried, it tightened and held the chair together. Unseasoned wood also was used to the same advantage. A dry round or stretcher would be driven into a "green" post and as the latter cured, it would draw securely around the round. These tricks were not particularly indigenous to Utah but seem to have been used in the construction of furniture on the frontier everywhere.

From the beginning, small quantities of milled hardwood lumber had been freighted into the valley from the west coast as well as the east, but the supply in no way met the demand. Consequently, it became the custom to order goods packed in hardwood cases, the cases themselves often being more valuable for the fine furniture they would become than the merchandise they contained. Hardwood wagon bottoms were particularly sought after by scavenging cabinetmakers.

As the Saints were "called" to settle outlying areas, a cabinet-maker, chairmaker, or a very versatile carpenter was selected to be among them. By virtue of his talents, he usually made coffins when necessary also. This avocation led naturally to the position of local undertaker, and the combination furniture dealer and undertaker was taken for granted in all communities. Even in Salt Lake City, furniture maker Henry Dinwoodey announced in 1864, "I shall, in a few weeks, have a complete stock of Undertakers' Trimmings from the States which will enable me to furnish Coffins on short notice and in the best Style of Workmanship."

One of the most ambitious resettlements directed by the Church was the Cotton Mission to southern Utah in 1861. On October 23rd of that year, the **Deseret News** reported:

In view of the great demand there will be for cotton and other products of a warmer clime than Great Salt Lake, in the event that the civil war in the east should continue for a number of years, it has been deemed expedient by the First Presidency to materially strengthen the settlements that have been made in Washington County and make others where facilities for doing so exist. To accomplish this, a company numbering over 300 men with their families have been either selected or have volunteered to go there this fall. . . .

This advance guard, representing some 200 from Salt Lake County alone, was primarily concerned with building, fencing and opening farms for cultivation the following spring. Among them were Willis Coplan (cabinetmaker),

William McMillan (chairmaker), and Frederick Pfister (turner). Some pioneers appear to have been excused or else to have returned shortly to the Salt Lake valley. Frederick Pfister, for example, was advertising his spinning wheels from his mill in Parley's Canyon by 1865.

Other Cotton Mission cabinetmakers included Benjamin F. Blake, a mattress, chair, and cabinetmaker who ultimately was in charge of upholstery work in the St. George Temple and Thomas Cottam who made many items of furniture, his chairs being distinguished by their woven fibre bottoms.

Many early Dixie settlers purchased their woven, rawhide-bottomed chairs from Samuel K. Gifford who set up shop in Springdale in 1862. Interestingly, Gifford's great-grandson, Newel K. Crawford, reproduced these chairs in Springdale from local fruitwood in the 1950s. To date, this appears to have been the only reasonably successful attempt to reproduce early Utah pieces commercially.

Sometime before 1855, Elijah Elmer had established a cabinetshop in the walled community of Parowan, Iron County. About 1863, the shop joined with the cooperative store, shoe shop, saddle and harness shop, tannery, sawmill, and flour mill to form the Parowan United Manufacturing and Mercantile Institution or, for short, PUMI. The cabinetshop was managed by James Connell and a variety of furniture was turned out from local woods. These items included congress (captains') chairs, rockers, sidechairs, lounges (Mormon couches), clerks' desks, center tables, work stands, chests, and cupboards. PUMI supplied, in fact, just about everything that went into pioneer homes and the coffins that went out of them. The cooperative flourished at least through the 1870s.

Meanwhile, the summer of 1859 saw the establishment of the first sawmill in Cache County in northern Utah. Esias Edwards and Leroy Kent built a mill with an upright saw which was driven by water diverted from the Blacksmith Fork River. The following summer, some sixty settlers were persuaded to relocate in the area to help protect the mill from Indian harassment. The community became known as Millville. Edwards also had a grist mill and molasses mill as well as being an apparently competent cabinetmaker and distiller. His "Valley Tan" satisfied the imbibers and his rawhide-bottomed chairs, stools, bedsteads, and other pieces furnished many pioneer homes in the northern counties.

By late 1860, there were four sawmills in operation in Cache County with others in the process of being built. Elsewhere in the Territory, the hand-powered pit saw was typical, but in water-rich Cache, sawmills generally were operated by water power. Although shingles, siding, moldings, and lumber for construction were the principal products of these mills, a few, such as those owned by Edwards and P. N. Petersen of Logan, produced much of the hardy furniture used in the area.

The coming of the railroad in 1869 augered boom or bust for Utah's furniture makers according to their adaptability. For the adaptable Henry Dinwoodey, already in the East buying factory-made hardwood furniture when the last spike was driven,* the railroad brought prosperity. These eastern Victorian pieces were displayed side by side with the products of his local shop—the former apparently not offering too much competition for the latter. Edward W. Tullidge in his 1886 **History of Salt Lake City** noted that Dinwoodey's "homemade furniture ranked on a par with States' goods and was seen from one end of the Territory to the other." Ultimately, however, local production stopped, but the business Dinwoodey founded more than a century ago survives today as one of the West's fine furniture stores.

Others were not so fortunate. Or so adaptable. The railroad, blamelessly enough, brought everything — hardwood and hardware and glass as well as the finished product. But the last, finished with mirrors and marble in the machine-sped new fangled fashion was more competition than many master craftsmen with only average business acumen could bear.

It was not that they weren't encouraged to keep up the good work. George Q. Cannon, editor, wrote in the **Deseret News** of August 12, 1868:

. . . Home manufacture must be extensively and persistently pursued. But by the railroad the raw materials can be imported when necessary, as cheap or cheaper than the manufactured article is now and can be manufactured here. Many citizens have been desirous of importing furniture finer than can be manufactured out of timber in this country. Many imported tables, chairs, etc., have proved very flimsy and unsuitable for our dry and trying climate. Timber and other material for the manufacture of household furniture can be imported and, when made up here from well-seasoned and judiciously selected materials by workmen who have a local reputation to maintain, they will be more serviceable. Chairs made here will not be unsafe to sit upon.

But the handwriting was on the wall, or better, the print was in the 1869 Salt Lake City directory, the first such publication in the Territory. Editorially

---

* The first transcontinental rail line was completed May 10, 1869, at Promontory Summit, Utah, when rails of the Central Pacific (from California) and the Union Pacific (out of Omaha) were joined with the ceremonial driving of the last or Golden Spike.

the directory commented, "The completion of the line of railroad through to Utah will have a tendency to open up several branches of business which have been comparatively unnoticed before. Among those will doubtless be the importation of furniture into that region."

This was endorsed by the advertisement of William W. Strong, No. 203 Randolph St., Chicago: "Having restocked my store with some of the Richest and Most Elegant Furniture ever offered in the West. My present facilities enable me to offer the same at GREATLY REDUCED RATES. Parties wishing New Furniture of the most staple, rich, modern, and unique styles, will do well to call before purchasing elsewhere."

The same 1869 directory listed seventeen cabinetmakers in Salt Lake City. The next issue, dated 1874, carried the names of three.

The United Order cooperatives, begun at the insistance of Brigham Young in St. George in 1874, kept home industry in general and furniture-making in particular going in the quasi-isolated communities until that institution's demise in the late 1880s. In January of 1876, the United Order Foundry Machine & Wagon Manufacturing Company was organized in Logan. Its product was saw-mills which it shipped, together with mill parts and shingle mills, throughout the Territory.

At the same time, the United Order Building and Manufacturing Company was organized there. This included Card & Sons' saw-, lath-, and shingle-mill and P. N. Petersen's planing mill. Presumably, the latter's furniture shop was included also. PUMI functioned in Parowan, as has been noted, and an 1875 account observed "a few men at work making furniture" at the United Order in Sevier County.

In Kane County's Orderville, the most successful of the United Orders thrived until 1886, the cabinetshop turning out pieces similar in type and style to those produced in the earliest Territorial days. Occasionally, however, a cabinet pediment might suggest some Victorian Eastlake influence. The longevity of the Orderville shop was due primarily to the unique success of that particular experiment in communal organization as well as to the area's remoteness from the railroad and other centers of commerce.

But for the most part, furniture-making in Utah followed the wagon train into the sunset. And for the same reason — the necessity was no longer there.

**T**he following directory of cabinetmakers includes those in the trade and related fields who, research has indicated, worked in Utah before 1870. Many, of course, continued making furniture for some time after that date. All available information relative to the trade has been included. Biographical information also is included if available, pertinent, and of probable interest.

Reference sources include the first (1869) Salt Lake City directory, microfilm copies of the **Deseret News** (1850-1870), county and local histories, and unpublished masters' theses. Most of this material is available in the library of the Utah State Historical Society and is identified by author and page number in parentheses following each entry. Reference to the **Deseret News Weekly** of September 23, 1857, for example, is listed (DN 9-23-57). The directory is indicated by (SLCD'69). The succeeding directory, published in 1874 and officially titled **Gazeteer of Utah & Salt Lake City Directory**, is listed here as (SLCD'74).

Perhaps without exception, all tradesmen listed were converts to the Mormon Church; therefore, further biographical information probably would be available from the Genealogical Society or Historical Department, The Church of Jesus Christ of Latter-day Saints, in Salt Lake City.

Name spellings were found to be whimsical. Henry Dinwoodey's page-long, column-wide ad in the **Deseret News** of the early 1860s ran for several issues with his name spelled "Dinwoody." Ramsay was as likely to be "Ramsey;" "Phister" was both that and "Pfister;" and variations in initials leave doubt that the person is the same.

Lots weren't numbered in Salt Lake City until 1883, so one often encounters such complicated addresses as "northside of 2nd South between 1st and 2nd East, two doors from the boarding house." Over the years, names of streets have been changed also. These include East Temple (now Main) and 1st East (now State). Current designations, if known, are given in parentheses. Addresses, unless otherwise noted, are presumed to indicate residence rather than place of business.

# DIRECTORY OF CABINETMAKERS

**ABBOTT,** .............. A child's ladderback chair with leather seat, made about 1855, is in the DUP Museum, Salt Lake City.

**AHLANDER, Anders Frederik,** Provo. Died 1921. Pioneer maker of carriages and fancy furniture. He specialized in carved woodwork. (WPA, 162; DN 10-16-1965)

**ALLEN, William L. N.,** Salt Lake City. Listed as a cabinetmaker on South Temple corner of Locust ("I" St.) in 1869 and as a carpenter at the same address in 1874. (SLCD'69; '74)

**BEAN, Joseph,** Salt Lake City. Pioneer of 1859. A crude, painted pine ladderback armchair is in the DUP Museum. Bean was listed as a carpenter in 1869 on 8th East between South Temple and 1st South. (SLCD '69)

**BELL, William,** Salt Lake City; Heber. Born March 12, 1816, Barnard Castle, Durham, England. Died March 24, 1886, Heber City. The son of a carpenter, young William was taken out of school "as soon as he could hold a hammer"[1] and worked with his father until 1833 when he moved to London and found employment as a cabinetmaker.

He married Jane Heslop the following year. The couple joined the Mormon Church in 1850 and immigrated to America on the "John M. Wood" in the spring of 1854, landing at New Orleans. They proceeded directly to West Point, Missouri, where they joined Capt. James Brown's company of 300 immigrants to the Salt Lake valley. The 42-unit wagon train suffered many hardships enroute, Bell himself having a severe attack of mountain fever. The party arrived in Salt Lake City on October 1, 1854.

Employed by Brigham Young as a furniture maker, Bell worked exclusively for Young for fifteen years, living in President Young's first home and working in Young's cabinetshop until his own shop was built sometime before 1859. Early records show William Bell as owner of the property on the northwest corner of South Temple and Walnut ("A" St.) which corresponds to one account locating "Cabinetmaker Bell's workshop . . . on the southeast corner of Brigham Young's land."[2] It was in this shop that Ralph Ramsay carved the eagle crest for Brigham Young's Eagle Gate.

William and Jane had no children. But shortly after their arrival in the valley, William married Jane Laidlow, a widow whom he met aboard ship, and they became the parents of five. Bell was a member of the militia dispatched to Echo Canyon to confront Johnston's Army in the late fall of 1857.

Making furniture for his patron apparently kept Bell busy. It appears he never advertised and except for his association with the Deseret Agricultural & Manufacturing Society fair in 1861, little professional mention was made of him. J. C. Little noted in 1855 that his Deseret Carriage and Furniture Depot had "just formed a connection with . . . William Bell, recently from London, the best and most experienced cabinetmaker and upholsterer in the Territory."[3] No more information has been found about this association.

The DUP Museum in Salt Lake City owns a Victorian Gothic breakfront secretary made by Bell for Brigham Young in 1856 and a chair made by him for Heber C. Kimball. There is also an octagon table which was exhibited at the Territorial Fair in 1858. This piece was made from the wood of the wagons that brought Brigham and Lorenzo D. Young to the valley in 1847. The table is inlaid with various lighter woods. Several other pieces are owned by the LDS Church and are in the Lion and Beehive houses.

Bell was a member of the furniture awarding committee of the D.A.&M. fair in 1861, the same year in which he won $3 for the best rocking chair. He also was director of the Cabinetmakers, Carvers, Turners, and Upholsterers Car in the July 4th parade that year.

Called to a mission in Heber City in 1869, Bell made furniture there until three years before his death. (Mortimer, 271[1]; Carter, 235[2]; DN 11-21-55[3], 9-11-61; 4-28-86; SLCD '69)

**BENSON, Peter,** Newton. Simmonds notes that Benson made furniture at his shop in Newton until the turn of the century. (Simmonds, 48)

**BERNTSON, Rasmus,** Cache Valley. Listed as a carpenter who made shuttles, desks, egg crates, etc. during the 1860s. (Dial, 1)

**BIRD, Edmund F.,** Salt Lake City. A member of the awarding committee of the D.A.&M. 1861 fair, Bird won awards the same year for best center table and best bedstead. He was listed in 1869 and 1874 as a "carver in wood" on 3rd South between 2nd and 3rd West. (SLCD'69, '74)

**BIRD & FOSTER,** Salt Lake City. Advertisement in the **Deseret News** of March 7, 1860, read: "Wanted: 1000 pounds of cast iron by Bird & Foster, Cabinet Makers and Turners, East Temple (Main) Street, opposite Bishop Hunter's residence." (DN 3-7-60)

**BIRD, James,** Salt Lake City. One James Bird was a cabinetmaker in partnership with Henry Dinwoodey, carpenter, about 1856-1858. Together they took refuge in American Fork Canyon from Johnston's Army in 1858 where, after repairing an old sawmill, they made shoe pegs and milled lumber during the summer. Bird apparently settled in Provo from where he was called as a member of the Cotton Mission to St. George. He is listed there in 1862. No further record is found, and it is possible he returned to Salt Lake City where the directories of 1869 and 1874 list a James Bird, cabinetmaker, on the south side of 2nd South between East Temple (Main) and 1st East (State). (SLCD'69, 74; Tullidge, 694)

**BISHOP, Darius,** Millville. See Campbell, Sam.

**BLAKE, Benjamin F.,** St. George. Born March 12, 1815, Blandford, Dorset, England. Came to America in 1853 and to St. George in 1861. Died March 9, 1884, St. George. Blake served an apprenticeship in England and appears to have been a member of the Cotton Mission to southern Utah. A mattress-, chair-, and furniture-maker, he was in charge of upholstery work in the St. George Temple. Together with Thomas Cottam, he designed and constructed much of the early furniture used in Utah's Dixie. Blake used wood or rawhide for chair bottoms in contrast to Cottam's rush. Residence was on the southeast corner of 1st South and 1st East, St. George. (Hafen; Miller, 148; Larson, 278)

**BOVACK, James,** Spanish Fork. An emigrant from Scotland in 1855, Bovack is known to have made a three-slat, ladderback armchair with seat of woven willows. (Hendrickson, 28)

**BROWNING, Jonathan,** Ogden. Made pedestal parlor tables from knotted poplar wood on Ogden's first water-powered lathe, located at 16th and Washington St. (DN 10-16-1965)

**BURNETT, David,** Tooele. Notice in **Deseret News** of July 6, 1864: "WANTED: A Wood Turner to run a Turning Lathe and Circular Saw, propelled by water power

—One who has knowledge of fitting up Furniture would be preferred." (DN 7-6-64)

**CAMPBELL, Sam,** Millville. A Cache Valley pioneer of 1859, Campbell and his brother, Joseph, built the first log cabin in Spring Creek (later Providence). Together with Darius Bishop, he installed a turning lathe and made rawhide bottomed chairs and other articles of furniture. (Hovey, 100; Ricks, 39)

**CAPENER, William,** Centerville; Salt Lake City. Davis County DUP lists a William Capener as one of Centerville's early carpenters (1848), and as one who made all kinds of furniture. This may or may not be the same William Capener of Salt Lake City who placed the following notice in the **Deseret News** of April 3, 1860: "NOTICE To The People of Utah. Wm. Capener, 13th Ward, is about leaving for the States on business. All those indebted to him are requested to settle immediately. A Large Assortment of FURNITURE on hand cheap for Cash, Lumber, or Provisions."

In 1863, Capener & Taylor, Builder and Contractors, Wholesale and Retail Furniture Warehouse, Furnishing Undertakers, etc., advised:

Having greatly enlarged our premises, we are prepared to contract for Buildings, either in part or entire, both in town and country. We shall keep on hand a good supply of sash, panel doors &c. Furniture of all descriptions constantly on hand. The public can be accommodated with Coffins on the shortest notice. We would return to our patrons our thanks, and invite those indebted to pay their bills. And we will try and accommodate those who wish to make our acquaintance with as good an article in our line as the material and facilities of the country affords. Wanted: one inch, one and a half and two-inch white pine lumber; 4x4 and 3x4 scantling, 2-inch cottonwood plank. We want 30,000 ft. at the old stand, 1st South St., one and a half blocks east of the Theater.

The 1869 directory listed William Capener, cabinetmaker, at 1st South between 2nd and 3rd East. (Davis DUP, 70; DN 4-3-60, 7-1-73; SLCD'69)

**CAST (E), E. M.,** Salt Lake City. The following notice appeared in the **Deseret News,** March 7, 1860:

CABINET WAREHOUSE. I wish to inform my friends and the public generally that I have secured to myself the services of Mr. Powell, an experienced

TURNER, and also that I always have on hand a variety of CABINETWARE—TABLES, BEDSTEADS, CHAIRS, &c., which will be sold at reasonable prices for grain, lumber, and provisions of all kinds. E. M. Cast, Half Block North of Emigration Street on State Road.

In 1869, E. M. Caste was listed as a furniture maker with shops on 1st East (State St.) between 2nd and 3rd South and residence at the corner of Chestnut ("B" St.) and Bluff (3rd Ave.) (DN 3-7-60; SLCD'69)

CLUFF, David Jr., Provo. An 1868 newspaper notice read: "Provo Cabinet Shop! David Cluff Jr., proprietor. Furniture constantly on hand. Cheap for Cash or Produce." An upholstered, scrolled Empire settee was illustrated. The Provo section of the 1874 directory listed Cluff as an "Importer and Manufacturer of furniture, bedding, and coffins of all kinds. Office and Wareroom, 2nd E. and Main St." (DN 3-28-68; SLCD'74)

CONNELL, James, Parowan. Emigrant from Scotland. In 1863, he managed the PUMI cabinetshop with Thomas Durham. (Dalton, 364)

COPLAN, Willis, St. George. Born in Virginia, Coplan lived in Texas and California before coming to Utah in 1858 and St. George in 1861. He was a carpenter, cabinetmaker, and turner. Residence was on the southeast corner of 3rd North and 2nd West. He became a horticulturist and moved to Beaver in 1869. (Hafen, 31)

COTTAM, John Sr., Salt Lake City. Cottam received the D.A.&M. award for the best 6-chair set in both 1860 and 1861 and for the best rocking chair in 1860. He was listed as a "chair mender" at 5th West between North Temple and 1st North in 1869 and 1874. (DN 10-17-60; SLCD' 69,'74)

COTTAM, Thomas Sr., St. George. Born October 18, 1820, Meadowland, Yorkshire, England. Died November 10, 1896, St. George. Cottam came to America in 1841; lived in Nauvoo, Illinois; arrived in Salt Lake City, 1852; and moved to St. George as a member of the Cotton Mission in 1861. A turner and chairmaker, he had served an apprenticeship in England. Cottam specialized in rush-bottomed chairs, gathering rushes from the marshlands along the Virgin River. Chairs usually had shaped stiles and ladder backs, the slats characteristically separated by three ball-shaped spacers in the Sheraton Fancy manner. They were made of native pine and grained to simulate fruitwood. Cottam's home was an adobe house on the northwest corner of Tabernacle and

2nd East, present site of the Washington County courthouse. (Cottam, 4; Hafen, 31; Kesler, 53; Larson, 278)

**COWLEY, William Michael,** Cache Valley. Manufactured frames and rush-bottomed chairs. (Dial, 2)

**CURTIS, Hyrum,** Cache Valley. Made chairs, saddletrees, and bottomed chairs in 1864. He was one of the founders of Newton in 1869. (Dial, 2; Ricks, 68)

**DAHLQUIST, Laurentius,** Salt Lake City. Dahlquist made fancy furniture, some of it for the Salt Lake Temple, and much of the cabinetwork and panelling for the Gardo House. (DN 10-16-1965; WPA, 162)

**DALLAS, Samuel B.,** Salt Lake City. Listed as a cabinetmaker at 1st West between North Temple and 1st North in 1869, 1874. (SLCD'69, '74)

**DELMORE & BRO.,** Ogden. Listed in 1869 as cabinetmakers at south end of Main. (SL CD'69)

**DINWOODEY, Henry,** Salt Lake City. Born September 11, 1825, Latchford, Cheshire, England. Died October 1, 1905, Salt Lake City. Dinwoodey's father was a blacksmith who died when Henry, the oldest son and second of five children, was thirteen. Henry had attended school intermittently and, at nine, had started work in a rope walk. He left this shortly for a job in a chandler's shop.

Upon the death of his father, however, Henry purchased some second-hand carpenter tools in nearby Liverpool and apprenticed himself to a builder at Warrington. When he was about nineteen, young Dinwoodey moved on to Newton-in-the-Willows where he found employment as a pattern maker in an iron foundry and where he boarded in a Mormon home. Here he accepted the faith and was baptized in 1845.

Returning to Warrington, he met, converted, and married Ellen Gore. Together with his brother John, the couple sailed from Liverpool for New Orleans aboard the "Berlin," September 5, 1849. They landed in New Orleans on October 23rd and remained there until the following spring. Dinwoodey worked as a carpenter for $3 a day (at that, four times what he had received in England) and ultimately joined one James Stevens in the manufacture of rainwater cisterns.

In April 1850, the family moved to St. Louis where they rented a small store at the corner of Sixth Street and Washington Avenue from which Ellen sold dry goods and notions while Henry became head pattern maker in Dowdell's Foundry.

Leaving St. Louis in May 1855, Henry and Ellen booked passage on a Missouri River steamboat to Atchison, Kansas. Here they purchased oxen and a wagon, which they loaded with salable merchandise, and set off for the West with Capt. John Hindley's independent company. They arrived at Salt Lake City about the middle of September.

The Dinwoodeys spent the winter in a rented room of a house at the corner of 3rd South and 1st West. The following spring they moved into a home built by Henry on an adjoining lot for which he had traded the oxen and wagon. Henry worked as a carpenter, subsequently entering into partnership with cabinetmaker James Bird (q.v.) whose shop was located on East Temple (Main) Street.

Henry Dinwoodey's Cabinet and Chair Shop, East Temple (Main) Street, Salt Lake City, in the 1860s. Note Mormon couch behind the gentleman on the right and sidechair on the roof. Other pieces displayed in front of the store include rocking chairs, congress chairs, and a spinning wheel. (Photo courtesy Utah State Historical Society)

As Orson F. Whitney tells it in 1904, "This partnership continued until the fall of 1857, when trade was prostrated by news of the approach of Johnston's Army. Mr. Dinwoodey joined the militia and helped to repel the invaders, serving first in a troop of lancers under Captain H. B. Clawson between Salt Lake City and Fort Bridger, and afterwards in an infantry company in Echo and Weber Canyons. He returned home in December. His appointment as captain of the infantry came twelve years later."

Johnston and his 3,000 federal troops were pressing on Salt Lake City in the spring of 1858 and the Dinwoodeys with partner Bird loaded their belongings into a borrowed wagon and headed for the hills. They spent the summer of exile in American Fork Canyon, some 35 miles to the southeast, where Dinwoodey and Bird milled lumber after repairing a saw- and gristmill they found there.

Dinwoodey was impressed with the availability of native pine in the nearby canyons and upon his return to the city in the fall of 1858 he, together with a partner named Olson, built a shop on the west side of Main Street between South Temple and 1st South where they began manufacturing furniture. Olson soon left to become a farmer and Dinwoodey continued the business alone.

The **Deseret News** of June 11, 1862, carried the following notice:

WANTED At H. Dinwoody's (sic) Furniture Warehouse, opposite the Telegraph Office, 26,000 feet of Lumber as follows: 8000 ft. of 2-in. White Pine, Cotton-wood or Quaking Asp Plank. 7000 ft. of 1-in. White Pine; 2000 ft. 1½ in. White Pine; 1000 ft. 2x4 White Pine; 4000 ft. 1x4 in. White or Red Pine. Also, about 30 or 40 cords of Red Pine or Quaking Asp Wood, for which I will exchange Furniture of all kinds, spinning wheels, etc.

Barter being a way of life on the frontier, Dinwoodey explained:

I was always on hand for a trade. Scarcely anything coming amiss — lumber, adobes, beef, provisions, boots and shoes, and even beet molasses and soft soap being taken in exchange. There was no regular pay-day, but whenever a man required anything, I would give him an order on some tradesman with whom I kept a credit account, exchanging my goods for his. I thus enabled many of my employees to obtain homes. When one of them stated to me that he wished to purchase a certain lot and build himself a house, I would trade for the land for him and give him an order on the lumberman, adobe maker, brick mason, etc., and by this means he would get his house built and would repay me in labor, which payment being complete, I would give him a deed for his property.*

About 1861, business had so increased that expansion was necessary. Dinwoodey bargained for a piece of land on the south side of 1st South between Main and West Temple, paying the owner, Thomas Bullock, for the property by fencing the remainder of Bullock's lot with a six-foot-high board fence. Still retaining his place on Main Street, Dinwoodey built an adobe workshop on the rear of the new property. Three years later, display rooms were added in front. Meanwhile, he purchased land to the east where an addition to the store was erected.

In 1864, Dinwoodey announced in the **Deseret News** of September 7th:

Extensive Cabinet Establishment! H. Dinwoodey. Having made important additions to my shops, and having on hand a Large Quantity of Seasoned Lumber for the Manufacture of every description of CABINETWARE, and being now engaged in further enlarging my work-shops and warerooms, I take pleasure in announcing to my friends and the public that I am prepared to fill orders to any amount in the line of Household Furniture. I shall, in a few weeks, have a complete stock of Undertaker's trimmings from the States which will enable me to furnish COFFINS on short notice and in the best Style of Workmanship. SHOPS: On East Temple St., opposite the Telegraph Office and on First South Street west of the Meat Market. WANTED: About 30,000 Feet Lumber, 4x4 Scantling, 12, 14, 16 feet long; White Pine, 3x4 . . .; 2-inch Cottonwood Plank; 2-inch White Pine; 1-inch White Pine.

The following year, 1865, new cabinet warerooms on East Temple Street were announced from which "A Choice Assortment of Good Household Furniture, Oil Painted, and made out of Well Seasoned Lumber," was available.

About 1866 in order to facilitate the manufacture of furniture, Dinwoodey sent east for a small, four-horsepower steam engine, the

---

*Whitney, 254.

first for such purpose in the Territory. He sold it before it arrived, however, having bought in the meantime a ten-horsepower engine that had been used in connection with oil well speculation on the Bear River. This powered his turning lathe, circular saw, drill, etc. until additional machinery could be brought in by rail.

Throughout the last half of the 1860s, Dinwoodey's furniture ads were the only ones in the trade appearing regularly in the **Deseret News.** These page-long, column-wide advertisements might have prompted the Business-Office-Must comments that ran in a local editorial column titled "Home Items." In the issue of June 14, 1866, the column noted:

Friend Dinwoodey apprises the public that he has a large assortment of furniture on hand and can do with a very large quantity of lumber. Bro. Henry turns out good work, and has a big establishment in full blast. Patronize him.

Henry Dinwoodey (light colored suit) in his First South furniture store some time after the carpet line was added in 1873. Much of the inventory at that time was imported by rail from the States including, most likely, the caned bentwood rocker in the foreground. (Photo courtesy Utah State Historical Society)

The August 23rd column added:

H. Dinwoodey is adding to his already extensive business premises a large building on First South St. He is so well known that comment is needless. His rapidly growing trade tells how the public appreciates his efforts. Friend Henry is great on cabinet business and can construct a bureau more elegant and durable than a great many political ones.

His inventory of furniture items was extensive. Advertised in February, 1867, were "Chairs: parlor, kitchen, Windsor, dining room, French; gentlemen's large easy rockers; ladies' sewing rockers; children's table high chairs, babies' small chairs and rockers. Bedsteads: French, extra and plain; Cottage, extra and plain. Lounges: double and single, scrolled and fancy. Tables: large extention, oval center, round center, fall-leaf breakfast, plain kitchen. Stands: square, round, and oval. Wardrobes, bureaus, clothes chests." Also included were easy rockers and oval-back nurse rockers from the States. This contradicts the report that no States-made furniture was imported into the Territory for sale until after the coming of the railroad.

As already noted, Dinwoodey was in New York City buying furniture and machinery when the transcontinental rail line was completed at Promontory, May 10, 1869. Once his orders arrived in Ogden, they were freighted to Salt Lake City by ox teams as the Utah Central Railroad to the capital city was not yet completed. This new machinery, including among other tools a planer and mortising and shaping machines, greatly facilitated the manufacture of furniture. The firm also did custom sawing, turning and planing. Dinwoodey's board-sided shop on East Temple (Main) was torn down in 1871 and a new two-story building was erected in its place. But even this expansion could not adequately accommodate the increasing trade. So the space was leased and the stock moved to the 1st South location, the site of the present business.

A portion of the adobe building there was demolished in 1873 and a new three-story brick structure added. This improvement enabled Dinwoodey to have the largest display of furniture between Omaha and San Francisco. A new factory and workshops were built also and a wallpaper and carpet inventory added. Eventually this was expanded to include hardware and crockery also.

His business prospering, Dinwoodey became a naturalized citizen in 1865 and a director of numerous enterprises during the 1870s and 1880s. He served as city alderman from 1876 until 1884.

Henry and Ellen Gore were childless. With his second wife, Anne Hill, he was the father of eight; and with the third, Sarah Kinnersley, one. During the 1885 crackdown on polygamists, Dinwoodey was arrested for "holding out" his wives, fined $300, and sentenced to six months in the penitentiary.

Dinwoodey's residence was listed on 1st West between 3rd and 4th South in the 1869 directory. (Burt, 26; DN as noted; Manley, 45; Tullidge, 151, 694; SLCD'69; Whitney, 252-256)

**DOMVILL, Thomas,** Salt Lake City. Listed as a joiner on 6th South between West Temple and 1st West, 1869. (SLCD'69)

**DOOLITTLE, John,** Salt Lake City. Listed as a furniture maker on West Temple between 3rd and 4th South in 1869. The 1874 directory named Ruth A. Doolittle, widow, at above address. (SLCD'69,'74)

**DURHAM, Thomas,** Parowan. In 1856 this English carpenter opened a cabinetshop in the basement of the old Parowan cotton factory. He joined James Connell in 1863 to manage the PUMI cabinetshop. (Dalton, 364)

**EDWARDS, Esias,** Millville. Born in Virginia; an expert mechanic. Together with Leroy Kent, Edwards built the first water-powered sawmill in Cache Valley on the Blacksmith Fork River in 1859. A grist mill, molasses mill, and distillery were soon added and the town of Millville grew around these enterprises. Edwards made chairs with rawhide bottoms, stools, beds, and other articles of furniture for the local and neighboring settlements. As more mills were established in the valley, Edwards sold his interests to the community and moved to St. George. (Hovey, 98, 100; Ricks, 160)

**ELMER, E.,** Parowan. An item in the **Deseret News,** January 4, 1855, noted: "The flouring mill of Messrs. George A. Smith & John Calvin Smith is nearly ready for operation. This stands within the walls and in the highest part of town. Just below this mill are E. Elmer's cabinet and C. C. Pendleton's machine shops which will be a great benefit to that community." (DN 1-4-55)

**ENGSTROM, John,** Salt Lake City. Listed as a cabinetmaker on the south side of 1st South in 1869. The 1874 directory placed his business in the 8th Ward on the west side of 2nd East between 3rd and 4th South. (SLCD'69, '74)

**ERUGER, John,** Salt Lake City. Listed as a cabinetmaker on 6th East, corner of 4th South, 1869. (SLCD'69)

**FALLON, Henry,** Salt Lake City. Listed as a cabinetmaker on South Temple, corner of 2nd East, 1869. (SLCD'69)

**FOSTER, William H.,** Salt Lake City. See Bird & Foster. The 1869 directory listed Foster as a cabinetmaker on the east side of East Temple (Main) below 2nd South. In 1874, his occupation was given as woodturner and his address as East Temple opposite Walker House. Residence was in the 7th Ward, west side of West Temple between 3rd and 4th South. (SLCD'69, '74)

**GARF & HAYES,** Cache Valley. Operators of a planing mill manufacturing doors, sashes, boxes, etc. (Dial, 2)

**GIFFORD, Samuel K.,** Springdale. Gifford's chairmaking business established in 1862 was one of the first commercial ventures in Springdale. His rawhide-bottomed chairs were made from timber cut in the Eagle Peaks Mountains. (Hendrickson, 16; Larson, 278; Washington DUP 285, 352)

**GRANT, Robert,** Salt Lake City. Listed as a cabinetmaker on 6th South between East Temple (Main) and 1st East (State) in 1869 and 1874. (SLCD'69, '74)

**HANCEY, James,** Hyde Park. Hancey came to Hyde Park in July 1860, only a few months after the first settlers. With Thomas Hillyard, he built a shingle mill in 1865 powered by water from the Logan-Richmond Canal. Later with George Parrott, he built a wood-turning lathe, subsequently adding a lathe for turning iron. This was used often in the repair of machinery. Hancey also made furniture including cupboards, chairs, beds, etc. and "helped to fit out many married couples." (Bird, 60; Hovey, 104)

**HANSEN, Eric(k),** Spanish Fork. A caned Grecian rocker made in Spanish Fork by Eric Hansen, cabinetmaker, is in the DUP Museum, Salt Lake City. (Hendrickson, 25)

**HANSON, John,** Salt Lake City. Listed as cabinetmaker in 1869 at 6th East, corner of 7th South. (SLCD'69)

**HARPER, Joseph S.,** Salt Lake City. Listed as a joiner in 1869 on 6th South between 6th and 7th East. (SLCD'69)

**HARRIS, John J.,** Centerville. A carpenter and one of the first settlers (1848) in the area, Harris owned a turning lathe and made wooden utensils such as rolling pins and potato mashers. His congress (captain's) chair made in the 1850s is illustrated in Mrs. Kesler's thesis. Harris was one of three carpenters who worked on the Centerville Ward, 1879-1882. (Davis DUP, 60, 70; Kesler, 57)

**HALVORSEN, Peter O.,** Salt Lake City. Listed as a cabinetmaker on West Temple between North Temple and 1st North in 1869. (SLCD'69)

**HENDERSON, David P.,** Salt Lake City. Listed as a joiner on 6th South between East Temple (Main) and 1st East (State) in 1869. (SLCD'69)

**HUDSON, Thomas N.,** Salt Lake City. Listed as a cabinetmaker on 2nd North between West Temple and 1st West in 1869 and on the east side of Central between Plum and Peach (19th ward) in 1874. (SLCD'69, '74)

**HUISH, Walter,** Payson. A native of England, Huish was sent to Payson by Brigham Young in 1853 to establish one of the first furniture factories in Utah. He also made coffins. (Hendrickson, 45)

**HULSE, James,** Salt Lake City. Listed as a woodturner on Spruce ("D" St.) corner of Prospect (4th Ave.) in 1869 and as a carpenter in 1874, residing in the 11th ward on the south side of 1st South between 6th and 7th East. (SLCD'69, '74)

**HUMES, Nathan,** Salt Lake City. Listed as a cabinetmaker on 7th South between 3rd and 4th East in 1869. (SLCD'69)

**HYDE, Joseph Edward,** Cache Valley. Listed as a cabinetmaker in 1869. (Dial, 3)

**IRVIN, Robert,** Salt Lake City. Listed as a cabinetmaker on 1st West between South Temple and 1st South, 1869. (SLCD'69)

**IVERSON, Jeppie,** ................ Hendrickson pictures a 3-slat ladderback chair with solid rawhide seat made by Iverson in 1856. (Hendrickson, 27)

**JACOBS, Andrew,** Salt Lake City. Listed as a cabinetmaker at Cherry ("L" St.) corner of Bluff (3rd Ave.) in 1869. (SLCD'69)

**JACOBSEN, Soren,** Bountiful. Born Denmark, 1852; arrived Salt Lake City, 1862; died in Bountiful, 1897. A skilled cabinetmaker and carpenter, Jacobsen kept his shop at the rear of the furniture store owned by Edward Thomas. He also made coffins and the railing that surrounds the stand in the Bountiful Tabernacle. (Davis DUP, 406)

**JONSON & LARSON,** Salt Lake City. Listed as cabinetmakers on the east side of East Temple (Main) below 2nd South, 1869. (SLCD'69)

**KIRKHAM, George,** Lehi. See Whipple & Kirkham.

**LANHAM, Thomas,** Salt Lake City. Listed as a woodturner on 1st South between 7th and 8th East, 1869. (SLCD'69)

**LARSEN & MAGLEBY,** Salt Lake City; Brigham City. A notice in the **Deseret News** of October 29, 1862, read: "Larsen & Magleby, Cabinetmakers. West Side of Main Street (Next to Jenkins Saddlers Shop). White pine lumber, quaking asp and red pine logs wanted in exchange for furniture." The issue of July 1, 1863, carried an illustration of a piano and sidechair and noted:

NEW ESTABLISHMENT, Larsen & Magleby, Cabinetmakers &c. West side of Main Street (next to Jenkins Saddlers Shop) Respectfully invite the continued patronage of their friends and the public generally to their present Establishment where all orders will be promptly filled and satisfactorily attended to at the most economical charges.

The same raw materials as above were requested. Two weeks later, "Complete Spinning Wheels and Reels always on hand" was added. From the **Deseret News** of May 24, 1865:

Cabinet Makers, Larsen & Magleby, Formerly of G.S.L. City, wish to inform the citizens of Box Elder County and Cache Valley that they have opened a Cabinet Shop in BRIGHAM CITY where they hope by good workmanship and strict attention to business, to merit a share of the public patronage. Furniture of all kinds on sale or made to order. Spinning wheels, complete, always on hand. Lumber wanted in exchange for Furniture.
(DN 7-1-63, 7-15-63, 5-24-65; Hendrickson, 19)

**LEITZ, Thomas,** Salt Lake City. Listed as a cabinetmaker at H. Dinwoodey's in 1869. (SLCD'69)

**LINCOLN, George,** Bountiful. Davis DUP notes Lincoln as a coffin-maker who also constructed, in 1857, the circular stairway leading to the gallery in the Bountiful Tabernacle. (Davis DUP, 406)

**LINDQUIST, Niels A.,** Cache County. Dial records Lindquist as being in the business of furniture making, upholstery, and woodenwares after 1868. An N. A. Lindquist, Main Street, Logan, is listed as a cabinetmaker and dealer in 1874. (Dial, 3; SLCD'74)

**LITTLE, Jesse Carter,** Salt Lake City. Born September 16, 1815, Belmont, Waldo Co., Maine; died December 26, 1893, Salt Lake City. Little was a member of the original company of pioneers in 1847 and a subsequent entrepreneur and wearer of many hats. Professionally, he seems to have considered himself a carriage, wagon, and sleigh manufacturer, but he also was city cemetery sexton, marshall of Salt Lake City, first chief of the volunteer fire department and, in 1874, proprietor of the American Hotel on the northeast corner of 2nd East and 1st South.

His notice in the **Deseret News** of November 21, 1855, read:

Deseret Carriage and Furniture Depot. J. C. Little (has) completed a workshop situated at his residence, 13th ward, one block east of Social Hall and (has) formed a connection with A. Monteeth of Boston, a first-rate practical carriage builder, and Wm. Bell (q.v.) recently from London, the best and most experienced cabinetmaker and upholsterer in the Territory. They will carry on above named business under the name and style of J. C. Little & Co. Furniture such as secretaries, bookcases, bureaus, bedsteads of every description and style, dining tables, center tables, card tables, and ladies' work tables. Chairs from $2.50 to $20 each. Sofas, couches, lounges, sideboards and every article in the cabinet line. Coffins furnished in six hours' notice. Our terms — Ready Pay Without Deviation.

By 1857, the business name was J. C. Little Furniture and Carriage Depot. Address was listed simply as 13th ward and pieces advertised included rocking, dining, and children's chairs, tables, lounges, and bedsteads. Carriages were manufactured and repaired, and ornamental painting was available on short notice. By summer of that year, the advertisement was trailed with "Wanted: 10 cords Quakingasp timber & 10,000 feet of lumber of various kinds. We will pay Furniture, Chairs, and City Scrip."

Little advertised common and dining chairs, congress and arm chairs, rocking and children's chairs, lounges, tables, bedsteads, etc., as being constantly on hand. He had a small grist mill also and "could grind grain for feed at short notice." Wheat and flour were taken in exchange for furniture.

At the D.A.&M. fair in 1860, Little was awarded $3 for the best bureau and a like amount for the best sofa. For placing second in the six-chair category, he received a diploma.

He appealed for one woodturner and two cabinetmakers "on bedsteads and tables" in January 1862; and by May of that year, he had entered into partnership with the Messrs. Hunt and Zitting:

. . . for the purpose of manufacturing extensively at J. C. Little's Machine and Work Shops, in the 13th Ward, every variety of Furniture and Cabinet Work, including Bureaus, Secretaries, Chests, Wardrobes, Tables, Washstands, Dressing Tables, Light Stands, Writing Desks, Bedsteads, Sofas, single and double Lounges, Cradles, Cribs, Boston and Common Rocking Chairs, Windsor and Common Flag-seat Chairs, Children's Small High and Rocking Chairs, French and Flag-seat Parlor Chairs, etc.

The same ad advised that the new firm would also manufacture doors, window sashes and blinds, spinning wheels, reels, swifts, flax spinning wheels, hay rakes, grain cradles, etc., and could "if required, manufacture PIANOS, having the materials on hand for the purpose and competent workmen to attend to that department." Pianos and other musical stringed instruments would also be repaired.

In exchange, Little, Hunt & Zitting would accept "cash, store orders, grain, flour, beans, beef, pork, lard, eggs, butter, molasses, cheese, wood, cloth, wool, cotton, livestock, and all kinds of valley produce which can be disposed of to enable us to carry on our business successfully."

Also acceptable were bedstead scantling, 4x4 and 3x4 inch pine; cottonwood and quaking asp plank, 2 inches thick and 16 inches wide; juniper of various widths, "chair stuff, table legs, common chair legs for turning, etc." Persons requiring doors, sashes, and blinds had to furnish their own lumber; and "As we intend to see a good article and as low as any house in this city, no credit will be given."

Throughout the period, Little's various businesses and residence were located in the 13th ward, 2nd East and 1st South. (DN 3-31-57, 6-17-57, 3-7-60, 1-29-62, 5-14-62; Hendrickson, 102; SLCD'69, '74)

**LIVSDALE, P.,** Salt Lake City. Listed as a cabinetmaker on West Temple between North Temple and 1st North, 1869. (SLCD'69)

**LUNDAHL, Peter A.,** Cache Valley. Manufacturer of woodenwares and furniture. (Dial, 3)

**MICHEAL, Thomas,** Salt Lake City. Listed as a cabinetmaker on Central between Currant and Apricot, 1869. (SLCD'69)

**MICHEALSON, William,** Salt Lake City. Listed as a cabinetmaker on 5th South between 6th and 7th East, 1869. (SLCD'69)

**NAISBE(I)TT, H. W.,** Salt Lake City. Born Yorkshire, England. Advertised in April 29, 1857, **Deseret News:** "Wanted a Cabinetmaker. An experienced woodman may find employment in the above business on application to W. Naisbett, 20th Ward. A young man will have preference." Henry E. Nesbilt (sic), cabinetmaker and clerk, 20th ward, Salt Lake City, is listed as one of the original Cotton Mission pioneers living in St. George in 1862. (DN 4-29-57, 8-23-57; Tullidge, 87, Washington DUP)

**OLSEN, Charles,** Cache Valley. A turner and maker of furniture and woodenwares in 1864. Charles Olsen was listed as a Logan cabinetmaker in 1874. (Dial, 4; SLCD'74)

**OUGHTON, Adam,** Salt Lake City. Listed as a chairmaker on North Temple between 6th and 7th West, 1869. (SLCD'69)

**PARRATT, George,** Salt Lake City. An item headed "Fine Workmanship" appearing in the **Deseret News,** October 7, 1868, noted that a desk made by George Parratt for A. W. Street and constructed of walnut, common white pine, and two kinds of cedar was "equal in artistic design and beautiful finish to any that would be turned out in a first-class New York establishment. All its parts harmonize and the polish and beauty which it displays show the skill and hand of a master workman." Parratt was listed as a cabinetmaker on 6th South between 4th and 5th West in 1869. This might have been the residence because the same directory placed G. Parratt & Sons, cabinetmakers, on the west side of East Temple (Main) below 2nd South. The 1874 directory listed George Parratt again in the 5th ward on the south side of 6th South between 4th and 5th West. (DN 10-7-68; SLCD'69, '74)

**PERRY, John,** South Bountiful. An 1849 settler in the community, Perry was an expert cabinetmaker and wheelwright whose home was well furnished with articles of his making. Among his pieces were tables, chairs, chests of drawers, cupboards, wagons and carts. (Davis DUP, 406)

**PETERSEN, P. N.,** Cache Valley. Bird notes that about 1865, Petersen built a planing mill across from Card's sawmill where he manufactured moldings, siding, and furniture. The business became part of the United Order Building & Manufacturing Co., January 10, 1876. Dial records that P. M. Peterson (sic), millman, made much of the early furniture used in the valley. (Bird, 59; Dial, 4)

**PETERSON, Charles,** Salt Lake City. Listed as a cabinetmaker on 7th East between 1st and 2nd South, 1869. (SLCD'69)

**PHISTER, Frederick,** Salt Lake City. A **Deseret News** account of October 12, 1865, notes:

> Bro. Frederick Phister is making flax and wool spinning wheels and patent wheelheads and doing general turning work at his establishment on the South Branch of Big Kanyon Creek (Parley's Canyon) near Bishop L. W. Hardy's eastern mail station. Br. Phister's prices are moderate and his work excellent as evidenced by some 2000 wheelheads and other evidences of his work throughout the Territory.

> Frederick Pfister (sic) of Salt Lake City, a turner, is recorded as one of the original Cotton Mission pioneers living in St. George in 1862. (DN 10-12-65; Washington DUP)

**PHELPS, Henry E.,** Salt Lake City. An advertisement in 1861 read: "For Sale, a full assortment of furniture kept constantly on hand, and made to order; also, a general Trading Store half block south of Council House." The 1869 directory lists Phelps' business as a "Variety Store" on the west side of East Temple (Main) between South Temple and 1st South. In 1874, he is recorded as a "dealer in dry goods and notions" at the same address. (DN 3-27-61; SLCD'69, '74)

**PINE, Horace,** Salt Lake City. Listed as a joiner on 3rd South, corner of 4th East, 1869. (SLCD'69)

**PORTER, Warriner,** Centerville. Pioneer of 1847. A pine bedstead made by Porter in 1862 of local wood and laced with rawhide strips is illustrated in the Kesler thesis. (Kesler, 40)

**PRICE,** ................., Salt Lake City. Listed as a cabinetmaker on the east side of East Temple (Main) below 2nd South, 1869. (SLCD'69)

**PULSIPHER, William,** Brigham City. A 1965 account notes that between 1853 and 1856, Pulsipher "patiently inlaid eagles in a chest of drawers for Christian and Hansena Hansen." He was the first permanent settler in Avon, 1880. (DN 10-16-1965; Ricks)

**QUIN, George,** Salt Lake City. Listed as a woodcarver on 6th East between South Temple and 1st South, 1869. (SLCD'69)

**RAMSAY, Ralph,** Salt Lake City; Richfield. Born January 22, 1824, Littlefell (near Ryton), Durham County, England. Died January 25, 1905, Snowflake, Arizona.

Apprenticed at age fifteen to a woodcarver and turner, Ramsay opened his own shop about the time he became a convert to the LDS faith in 1849. Once in America, he built handcarts for the trek west and arrived in Salt Lake City with the first handcart company in 1856.

Ralph Ramsay (1824-1905). Owner: Ettene Ramsay

Painted pine Sheraton Fancy sidechair shown with pedestal base parlor center table, the latter made by Ralph Ramsay of native woods from various localities. Red cedar for table's round top was taken from West Mountain near Richfield. Owner: Melissa Cluff

Footboard of Ralph Ramsay's elaborately carved bed. Piece was constructed over the period 1860-1887 in Utah, Arizona, and Old Mexico. Detail includes beehive finials, birds, rabbits, and seven different dogs' heads. (Photo courtesy Deseret News) Owner: Daughters of Utah Pioneers

Eagles and beehives became his specialty, and he is particularly noted for carving, in 1859, the original eagle for the Eagle Gate. Wooden oxen, models for the cast figures that support baptismal fonts in LDS temples, were carved by Ramsay. He was responsible also for the elaborate casework of the Salt Lake Tabernacle organ, the ornate woodwork in the old Salt Lake Theater, and woodwork and furniture for the Beehive and Lion Houses. His mantlepiece won first place as the best specimen of woodcarving exhibited at the D.A. & M. fair in 1860.

A **Deseret News** notice of August 26, 1863, read:
Ralph Ramsay, WOOD CARVER AND TURNER, Having fitted up machinery

Walnut corner etagere made by Ralph Ramsay. Owner: Ettene Ramsay

Dropfront secretary on cupboard base made by Ralph Ramsay, Richfield, about 1875, of pine and juniper from West Mountain. Piece has its original red cedar finish. Owner: Ettene Ramsay

Pedestal base detail of round-top parlor table carved by Ralph Ramsay of native woods from various localities. Flower and leaf motif on bracket knees. Owner: Melissa Cluff.

in the house lately occupied by President B. Young's Wool-Carding machine on City Creek, is now prepared to execute all kinds of Carving and Turning. Columns for Porticos, Verandahs, Halls, Galleries, etc., Turned and Carved to order. Country orders attended to. R. Ramsay, 20th Ward, G.S.L. City.

The 1869 directory lists Ralph Ramsay, woodcarver, at the corner of Fruit (1st Ave.) and Fir ("E" St.). In October 1872, he and his family moved to Richfield where he had been called by Brigham Young to help colonize and build houses and furniture for the settlers. His own home at 57 East 2nd North, still owned by a descendant, was built between 1872-1874 and furnished with pieces of his own making. His workshop where coffins and furniture were made was on the second floor. Ramsay kept at his trade until shortly before his death, a family legend claiming that he wore off his beard

Painted pine mantlepiece carved by Ralph Ramsay for his Richfield home about 1873. Owner: Ettene Ramsay

by bracing the chisel handle against his chin. He also made his own coffin several times before having need of it at age 81.

Ramsay made his furniture of wood found wherever he happened to be. Of particular significance is a much-traveled bedstead now the property of the DUP Museum in Salt Lake City. This piece was begun in Salt Lake in 1861 and added to in central Utah, Arizona, and Old Mexico of native woods found in each place.

A rococo umbrella stand was made for President Young's office about 1858 of native mountain mahogany with motifs of roses, grapes, and entwined vines surmounted by an antlered deer's head. Family pieces, however, are considerably more restrained. (DN 8-26-63, 10-30-1963; Hendrickson, 32; Jacobson, 163; SLCD'69)

**RAYBOULD, William.** Salt Lake City. Listed as a foreman at Dinwoodey's Furniture Factory, 1869. (SLCD'69)

**RILEY, J. S.,** Salt Lake City. An 1854 advertisement read:

Grecian, Windsor, and Fancy Chair Manufactory. J. S. Riley respectfully informs the public that he has commenced the above business on West Temple St., 2 doors south of Mr. Thos. Bullock's; that he has been preparing turned stuff most of the winter and spring, and has on hand a large lot of the best quality and well seasoned, that he will use the best finishing that can be obtained. Persons purchasing from him may be assured they will have a substantial article. Bedsteads, Tables, Lounges, &c., made to order. (DN 1-12-54)

**SCHEIB, John P.,** Salt Lake City. Listed as a cabinetmaker on South Temple between 3rd and 4th East, 1869. (SLCD'69)

**SCOFIELD, Joseph,** Salt Lake City. Listed as a joiner at 1st South between 1st (State) and 2nd East, 1869. (SLCD'69)

**SEVY, Buttler,** Toquerville. A 3-slat ladderback chair with rawhide thong seat attributed to Sevy is in the DUP Museum, Salt Lake City.

**SIDDALL, C. W.,** Salt Lake City. The following appeared in the **Deseret News,** January 19, 1854:

New Cabinet & Chair Shop. The undersigned would respectfully inform the citizens of Deseret that he has commenced the above business in the 12th Ward, one door East from Mrs. Fernham's boarding house; and by the use of good materials and moderate prices he hopes to gain a liberal share of public patronage. Produce, the best quality lumber, and maple wood in payment. And as the nimble ninepence is preferable to the slow shilling, Cash customers are politely invited to give me a call. C. W. Siddall. Small turning neatly done, and stirrups always on hand. (DN 1-19-54)

**SKIDMORE, Samuel,** Salt Lake City. Listed as a cabinetmaker on 1st South between West Temple and 1st West, 1869. (SLCD'69)

**SLAUGHTER, Samuel,** Salt Lake City. Listed as a turner at the corner of Beet and Short in 1869. (SLCD'69)

**SMITH & CO., Jno.,** Salt Lake City. A notice in the August 22, 1860, **Deseret News** advised that this firm had established a water-power turning lathe on the corner west of Temple Block on North Temple Street in the 17th Ward and was ready to supply customers with spinning wheels, clock reels, etc. (DN 8-22-60)

**SMITH, William,** Salt Lake City. An 1863 **Deseret News** ad read:

CHAIR MAKING IN THE 11th WARD. Wm. Smith has on hand Windsor, Rush-bottom, Rocking, Sewing and other chairs of the best workmanship. Call and see me and bring your Lumber, Produce, Home-made cloth, etc. My shop will be found one block and a half east and half block north of the Twelfth Ward School House. Wanted — 5000 feet 2-inch Cottonwood, Quaking Asp and White Pine Plank.

The W. J. Smith, Chair and Furniture Establishment, 11th ward, advertised moderate terms in 1865; and a **Deseret News** "Home Item" two years later observed: "Furniture: W. I. (sic) Smith of the 11th Ward Chair Factory offers furniture for produce, provisions, etc. Give him a call." William J. Smith was listed as a cabinetmaker on 6th East between South Temple and 1st South in 1869. (DN 8-26-63, 2-15-65, 4-5-65, 2-6-67; SLCD'69)

**SNIDER, S. C.,** Salt Lake City. Advertised in 1860: "WOOD TURNER WANTED IMMEDIATELY! Apply to S. C. Snider, 14th Ward." (DN 3-7-60)

**SPERRY, Charles,** Salt Lake City. The earliest chair extant made in Utah has been attributed to Charles Sperry. Constructed of native juniper from Little Cottonwood Canyon during the winter of 1847-1848, this rocker has a 4-slat ladderback and woven rawhide thong seat. Original owner was Mary Pitchforth. The chair is now in the DUP Museum, Salt Lake City. (Hendrickson, 24)

**STOFFERS, C. T.,** Salt Lake City. Listed as a cabinetmaker on 1st South between East Temple (Main) and 1st East (State), 1869. (SLCD'69)

**TAYLOR, Jabez,** Salt Lake City. Listed as a joiner on Mountain, corner of Fir ("E" St.), 1869. (SLCD'69)

**THORNBURG, Frederick,** Salt Lake City. Listed as an upholsterer on 4th East corner of 5th South, 1869. (SLCD'69)

**TOWNSEND, John,** Salt Lake City. Listed as a turner on 5th West between 5th and 6th South, 1869. (SLCD'69)

**TRESEDER, Richard M.,** Salt Lake City. Listed as a cabinetmaker on West Temple between 2nd and 3rd South, 1869. (SLCD'69)

**WELLS, James,** Salt Lake City. Listed as a cabinetmaker on the east side of East Temple (Main) between 2nd and 3rd South, 1869. (SLCD'69)

**WHIPPLE & KIRKHAM,** Lehi. Partnership of George Kirkham, carpenter, and Edson Whipple, member of a woodworking family. Pair is known to have produced Dixie rockers. (Boston, 180)

**WHITTAKER, Thomas,** Centerville. One of the first settlers of Centerville in 1848, Whittaker was an accomplished cabinetmaker, carpenter, scenery designer, band organizer, nurseryman, and the first silkworm grower in Utah. He was awarded the $2 first prize for the best lady's workbox at the D.A.&M. fair, October 1861. A low, contour-back nurse rocker and cradle made by Whittaker in 1859 are illustrated in the Kesler thesis. (Davis DUP, 60, 70-72; Kesler, 27)

**WILKINSON, Moses,** Salt Lake City. Listed as a woodturner on 9th East, corner of South Temple, 1869. (SLCD'69)

**WILLIAMS, Charles W.,** Salt Lake City. Listed as a cabinetmaker on 5th South between 2nd and 3rd East, 1869. (SLCD'69)

**WINEGAR, A.,** Salt Lake City. Listed as a cabinetmaker on North Temple between 3rd and 4th West, 1869. (SLCD'69)

**ZETTON, Charles E.,** Salt Lake City. Listed as a cabinetmaker on West Temple between North Temple and 1st North, 1869. (SLCD'69)

# BIBLIOGRAPHY

Bird, Douglas M. **A History of Timber Resource Use in the Development of Cache Valley, Utah.** Logan: Utah State University, 1964. M.S. in Forest Management. (Unpublished thesis).

Boston Museum of Fine Arts. **Frontier America: The Far West.** Boston: The Leether Press, 1975.

Burt, Olive Woolley. "Founder of Tradition,A Story of Utah's Furniture Development," **The Utah Magazine,** July 1946.

Carter, Kate B. **Heart Throbs of the West.** Salt Lake City: Daughters of Utah Pioneers, 1939.

Cottam, Charles Walter. **Autobiography of Charles Walter Cottam: Lest I Forget to Remember.** Provo: J. Grant Stevenson, 1968.

Dalton, Luella Adams. **History of Iron County Mission and Parowan the Mother Town.** Private, c. 1963.

Davis County Company, Daughters of Utah Pioneers. **East of Antelope Island.** Salt Lake City: Publishers Press, 1948.

Dial, Willis A. **A Study of the Early Industrial Development in Cache Valley.** Logan: Utah State University, 1951. M.S. in Education. (Unpublished thesis).

Goeldner, Paul. **Utah Catalog Historic American Buildings Survey.** Salt Lake City: Utah Heritage Foundation, 1969.

Hafen, A. K. **Devoted Empire Builders.** St. George: Private, 1969.

Hendrickson, James Lewis. **A Pictorial Presentation of Furniture Manufactured in Utah, 1847-1957.** Logan: Utah State University, 1960. M.S. in Industrial Arts Education. (Unpublished thesis).

Hovey, Merlin R. **An Early History of Cache County as Printed in Logan Journal, 1923-25.**

Jacobson, Pearl F., ed. **Golden Sheaves From a Rich Field.** Richfield: Richfield Reaper Company, 1964.

Kesler, Bonnie Adams. **Utah Pioneer Homes— Interior Decoration & Pioneer Objects.** Salt Lake City: University of Utah, 1950. M.A. (Unpublished thesis).

Knecht, William L. and Crawley, Peter L. **History of Brigham Young, 1847-1867.** Berkeley: MassCal Associates, 1964.

Larson, Andrew Karl. **I Was Called to Dixie.** Salt Lake City: Deseret News Press, 1961.

Manley & Litteral, ed. **Utah, Her Cities, Towns and Resources.** Chicago: Manley & Litteral, 1891-2.

Miller, Albert E. **The Immortal Pioneers, Founders of the City of St. George, Utah.** Private, 1946.

Mortimer, William James. **How Beautiful Upon the Mountains, A Centennial History of Wasatch County.** Wasatch County Chapter, Daughters of Utah Pioneers, 1963.

Reid, Hyrum Lorenzo. **Early History of Utah's Dixie.** Provo: Brigham Young University, 1931. M.S. (Unpublished thesis)

Ricks, Joel E. **The History of a Valley (Cache).** Logan: Cache Valley Centennial Commission, 1956.

Sloan, Edward L. **Gazeteer of Utah & Salt Lake City Directory.** Salt Lake City: Salt Lake Herald Publishing Company, 1874.

Sutton, Wain, ed. **Utah, A Centennial History,** Vol. I. New York: Lewis Historical Publishing Co., Inc., 1949.

Simmonds, A. J. **The Big Range: A History of Cornish, Trenton, Clarkson, Newton, and Amalga, Utah.** Logan: Utah State University, 1967. M.A. in History. (Unpublished thesis).

Tullidge, Edward W. **History of Salt Lake City.** Salt Lake City: Star Printing Company, 1886.

Walker, Vance D. **History of Hyrum, Utah.** Hyrum, 1944.

Washington County Chapter, Daughters of Utah Pioneers. **Under Dixie Sun.** Panguitch: Garfield County News, 1950.

Whitney, Orson F. **History of Utah,** Vol. IV. Salt Lake City: George Q. Cannon & Sons Company, 1904.

Works Progress Administration. **Utah, a Guide to the State.** New York: Hastings House, 1941.

1. One of the first amenities in a new cabin, a bedstead, sprung with ropes or rawhide, was built into a corner. Posts and rails were crude, often with the bark still on. This double-decker was a space saver. (Pioneer Village, Salt Lake City)

2. This Morris chair, made by William Bell for Heber C. Kimball in the 1860s, predates the general acceptance of the style in America by some twenty years. Wood is painted dark brown; upholstery is red and tan plush. (Photo courtesy of Index of American Design)

3. Single lounge (Mormon couch) of native pine with turned spindles. Owner: Utah State Parks & Recreation Dept.

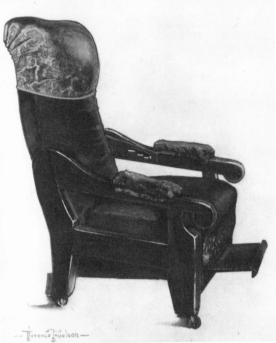

4. Single lounge (Mormon couch) of native pine with turned spindles. Scrolled crest rail and arm supports are in the Country Empire manner. Southern Utah provenance.
Owner: Utah State Parks & Recreation Dept.

5. Double lounge (Mormon couch) closed. Scrolled crest rail and arm supports are in Country Empire style. This piece was made of native Ponderosa pine, painted and decorated, in the United Order cabinetshop, Orderville, c. 1878. (Pipe Spring National Monument)

6. Alternating slats in the platform allow the double lounge (Mormon couch) to become a double bed. This piece of native pine was grained to simulate oak.
Owner: Utah State Parks & Recreation Dept.

7. This double lounge (Mormon couch) was made of pine and grained with paint to simulate hardwood by an unidentified cabinetmaker in Salt Lake City, last half 19th century. (Photo courtesy Corporation of the President of The Church of Jesus Christ of Latter-day Saints)

8. This Dixie rocker, an interpretation of the Boston rocker, was made in St. George in 1874 by the Builders' Union especially for Elder George A. Smith. The piece is larger than most, but the squared and contoured bannisters, heavy splayed legs with inset rockers, and slightly shaped plank seat are typical of similar chairs, generally referred to as "gentlemen's large rockers," made in most early Utah cabinetshops. Wood is Ponderosa pine, stained red.
Owner: Utah State Parks & Recreation Dept.

9. Flour boxes, capable of holding 1,000 pounds of flour, were standard kitchen items. Top was in two sections — a flat, fixed surface at the back and a hinged, sloping flap at the front. Corners often were joined by dovetailing. Owner: Kenneth J. Capelle

10. Decorated pine armchair with rush seat has distinctive ball-shaped spacers, a feature found on many Sheraton Fancies made in the eastern states during the first quarter of the 19th century. This piece was painted dark brown and decorated with yellow paint simulating banding. The chair was part of the original furnishings of the St. George Temple and could have been made there by Thomas Cottam. Matching pieces have been found in Salt Lake City, however, indicating a standard cabinetshop design. (Pipe Spring National Monument)

11. Pine rocker attributed to Brigham Young. Ball-shaped spacers were a feature of many eastern Sheraton Fancies in the early 19th century. This rocker was found in southern Utah. Its original seat was rush and the piece bears a striking similarity to Figure 12, a doll's chair made in St. George by Thomas Cottam.
Owner: Utah State Parks & Recreation Dept.

12. Doll's rocker with rush seat and shaped stiles, 24 inches high, was made in St. George by Thomas Cottam. Pine, painted black. (Pipe Spring National Monument)

13. Design and manufacture of this pine commode, made in Salt Lake City during the 1850s, have been attributed to Brigham Young. Painted graining on the base simulates hardwood while top and splashboard are glazed in imitation of green marble. Piece is 33½ inches high and 31 inches wide. Style is Country Empire. (Photo courtesy Index of American Design)

14. Empire sofa made about 1856 is believed to have been designed by Brigham Young and made in his cabinetshop, Salt Lake City. Ornately carved wood is grained to simulate mahogany. Piece is 7½ feet long by 4 feet, 1½ inches high. Upholstery is velvet. (Photo courtesy Index of American Design)

15. Octagon shaped, four-place clerks' desk of native pine grained to simulate walnut, made in Salt Lake City by Public Works. Writing surfaces are topped with leather. The design of this unique piece is attributed to Brigham Young. It was used by him, his two counselors, and a secretary. (Photo courtesy Corporation of the President of The Church of Jesus Christ of Latter-day Saints)

16 (a). Empire gondola sidechair of native pine. The design is attributed to Brigham Young. Graining on this piece shows less professionalism than usual. It was made in the Public Works cabinetshop, Salt Lake City, and is stamped on the bottom "PUBLIC WORKS, 1856, G.S.L. CITY." Many chairs of similar design were made with variations only in width of seat and back and in length and splay of legs. (Photo courtesy Corporation of the President of The Church of Jesus Christ of Latter-day Saints)

16 (b). Underside of chair seat shows stencil used by Public Works and identifies year of manufacture. (Photo courtesy Corporation of the President of The Church of Jesus Christ of Latter-day Saints)

17. A single piece of rawhide with hair remaining served the dual purpose of providing seat and holding the frame together. The natural curing process of either the rawhide or green wood caused this juniper ladderback to warp.
Owner: Utah State Parks & Recreation Dept.

18. Woven rawhide strips form back and seat while securing frame of this southern Utah juniper sidechair. The piece is a reproduction made about 1961 by Willard O. Hamblin for the restored Jacob Hamblin home in Santa Clara. Owner: Utah State Parks & Recreation Dept.

19. Thin rawhide thongs in an open weave was a common method of bottoming chairs.
Owner: Utah State Parks & Recreation Dept.

20. Decorated pine rocker with rawhide thong seat made in United Order cabinetshop, Orderville, c. 1875-1885. This piece was restored in 1959. It is not known if the original decorations were copied. (Pipe Spring National Monument)

21. Any hardwood was eagerly converted into furniture in the early days. This oak drop-leaf table top came to Utah as the bed of a Conestoga wagon. The table was made in Salt Lake City about 1850 and used in the family dining room of the Beehive House. Legs and braces were made of native pine. (Photo courtesy Corporation of the President of The Church of Jesus Christ of Latter-day Saints)

22. Detail of underside construction. (Photo courtesy Corporation of the President of The Church of Jesus Christ of Latter-day Saints)

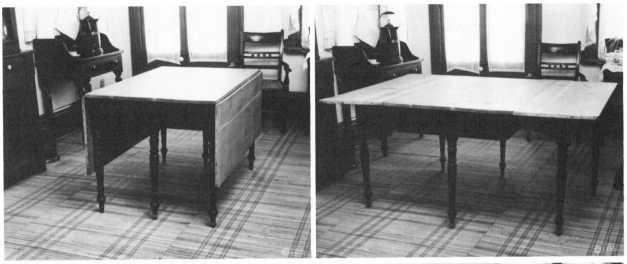

23. Walnut desk chair made in Salt Lake City about 1865 of walnut freighted into the Territory from the East. Upholstery is black horseshair, also imported from the States. This piece was used by Brigham Young in the Church office. (Photo courtesy Corporation of the President of The Church of Jesus Christ of Latter-day Saints)

24. Rope bed of the late 19th century. (Stagecoach Inn, Fairfield.)
Owner: Utah State Parks & Recreation Dept.

25. Rope bed used in southern Utah. Note screws on footpost for tightening ropes.
Owner: Utah State Parks & Recreation Dept.

26. Late 19th century pine bed, southern Utah provenance. Posts are composed of three vertical sections laminated together and rounded with a draw-knife.

Owner: Utah State Parks & Recreation Dept.

27. Plank-bottom Windsor sidechairs like these made up the popular six-chair sets produced by most Utah cabinetshops in the 1860s and 1870s. Chairs customarily were set back-to-table until after prayers had been said. Owner: Utah State Parks & Recreation Dept.

28. Splat-back sidechair with shaped plank seat and heavy, splayed legs. Similar pieces of local softwood, usually painted, were made everywhere in the Territory. (Pipe Spring National Monument)

29. Empire gondola sidechair, painted and with decorated splat, was a product of one of the more sophisticated cabinetshops of the Territorial period. (Photo courtesy LDS Church Information Office)

30. Armless Windsor nurse rocker with rolled seat in three sections, painted black with stenciled design on crest rail.
Owner: Utah State Parks & Recreation Dept.

31. Painted and decorated bent-arm Pennsylvania rocker with rolled seat was made in southern Utah of local softwoods, last quarter 19th century.
Owner: Utah State Parks & Recreation Dept.

32. Splat-back Pennsylvania rocker painted and decorated with landscape scenes. Rolled seat is in two sections joined at back cove. Piece was made in southern Utah, probably Orderville, of native softwoods. (Pipe Spring National Monument)

33.  Pine washstand of northern Utah provenance. Variations of this design were made by most cabinetshops.
Owner: Kenneth J. Capelle

34. Pine washstand, northern Utah, late 19th century. Portrait above is labeled "John Weggeland by his father Dan Weggeland, 1867." Danquart Weggeland (1827-1918) was a prominent Utah painter.
Owner: Kenneth J. Capelle

35. Pine nightstand produced in northern Utah, late 19th century. Porcelain knob might be a replacement as these customarily were wooden. (Honest Jon's Antiques)

36. Pine bureau with scrolled skirt, late 19th century.
Owner: Utah State Parks & Recreation Dept.

37. Small pedestal table with tripod base made of pine, probably in Salt Lake City, and originally painted black. Round top is composed of three boards laminated together.
Owner: Kenneth J. Capelle

38. One-drawer pine blanket chest with scrolled skirt probably made in northern Utah. Originally painted. (Honest Jon's Antiques)

39. Pine kitchen cupboard, 83 inches high, 18½ inches deep, 40 inches wide. Remnants of original milk- or lard-base stain remain. This piece probably was made in the Salt Lake valley. (Honest Jon's Antiques)

40. Victorian Eastlake slanted dropfront secretary made of pine in Salt Lake City during the 1860s. Original painted finish simulated hardwood. This massive piece, 102 inches tall, had been used as a kitchen cupboard in an adobe home in the northwest section of Salt Lake City. (Honest Jon's Antiques)

41. Pine corner cupboard made in Salt Lake City probably during the 1850s. Glass panels in upper doors. Painted graining simulates tiger and birdseye maple. (Photo courtesy Corporation of the President of The Church of Jesus Christ of Latter-day Saints)

42. Trestle-base painted pine clerk's desk with fixed slant top; southern Utah provenance, late 19th century.
Owner: Utah State Parks & Recreation Dept.

43. Dropfront pine clerk's desk on table base attributed to Public Works, Salt Lake City, c. 1850. Carved pine ornamentation is applied to dropfront exterior. Writing surface is leather-covered. Several such desks were used side by side in the Church offices. (Photo courtesy Corporation of the President of The Church of Jesus Christ of Latter-day Saints)

44. Tall pine dropfront station master's desk, southern Utah, late 19th century. Desk was used by telegrapher.
Owner: Utah State Parks & Recreation Dept.

45. Trestle-base dropfront pine clerk's desk made in the United Order cabinetshop, Orderville, by Isaac Carling about 1877 and used in the organization's office. Original golden oak finish. Cupboard interior is lined with patterned wallpaper. (Pipe Spring National Monument)

46. Painted pine clerk's desk with fixed slant top; one drawer in base, three in waist. Writing surface and medallions are painted to simulate burled walnut veneer. Central Utah provenance, late 19th century. (Honest Jon's Antiques)

47. Detail of 46.

48. Victorian Eastlake pine wardrobe grained to simulate walnut and attributed to William Bell, Salt Lake City. (Photo courtesy Corporation of the President of The Church of Jesus Christ of Latter-day Saints)

49. Painted pine sidechair in Sheraton Fancy style with rush seat, attributed to Thomas Cottam, St. George, 1860s. (Pipe Spring National Monument)

50. Detail of rawhide thong chair bottom, 13 by 16 inches. Chair was made in United Order cabinetshop, Orderville, 1875-1885, and was restored in 1959. (Pipe Spring National Monument)

51. Kitchen Windsor sidechair, usually part of a six-chair set, is typical of pieces produced by most Utah cabinetshops during the late 19th century.
Owner: John Edwards.

52. Double lounge (Mormon couch) with spool-turned arms, spindle back, and scrolled crest.
Owner: George Wilcox.

53. Rope bed made of pine in United Order cabinetshop, Orderville, about 1880. White painted swing cradle is from the Santa Clara area and might have been made there, but the design is that of a standard mail-order piece about the turn of the century. (Pipe Spring National Monument)

54. Pine bedstead with simulated birdseye maple graining made by United Order cabinetshop, Orderville, c. 1880. That's a bullet hole in the foot-board. (Pipe Spring National Monument)

55. Detail of headboard.

56. Hand-powered wood-turning lathe used in southern Utah. (Pipe Spring National Monument)

57. Painted pine mantlepiece simulating gray-veined white marble in dining room of Brigham Young's winter home, St. George. Owner: LDS Church.

58. Close-up of mantlepiece.

59. Detail of unrestored door frame showing original simulated oak graining on pine — an example of glazing by Brigham Young in his own home, Nauvoo, Illinois, about 1843.

60. Turned spindle pine rocker with rush seat; brown milk-paint finish. Chair is believed made in Utah about 1850.
Owner: Utah State Parks & Recreation Dept.